CART FOR A CAUSE COOKBOOK

PRESENTED BY LEXUS

D1445182

CART FOR A CAUSE COOKBOOK

PRESENTED BY LEXUS

BENEFITTING ST. VINCENT MEALS ON WHEELS

PHOTOGRAPHY BY DANA HURSEY

The Junior Advisory Board of
St. Vincent Meals on Wheels and founders
of Cart for a Cause dedicate this cookbook to
the more than 3,000 clients who receive hot,
nutritious meals every day—
SERVED WITH LOVE.

contents

acknowledgments

It took many hands and many hearts to make the dream of this cookbook a reality. We are forever grateful to Ralph Fowler and Dana Hursey for their belief in this project and for their support guiding us through it. Both have brought their wonderful eye, style, and creativity to the project. We are incredibly blessed that Rick Llanos made the introduction of Ralph and Dana to the project and acted as the link to make it happen and has always been there. Our gratitude goes to the creative team and colleagues who helped put this book together; it is theirs as much as ours. They all brought their dedication to the mission of St. Vincent Meals on Wheels and Cart for a Cause, their enthusiasm, and countless hours of hard work to the project. We sincerely thank Liz Anderson and the Department of Graphic Sciences, Dylan Borgman, Lisa Carney, Lourdes Claravall, Andrew Johnston, Bing Lacson, Damie Poonoosamy, Terri Robison, Jacob Rushing, Jennifer Sommer, Source Print Media Inc., Sarah Weaver, Anthony Wright, and all the chefs who have participated in Cart for a Cause.

We cannot thank Lexus enough for their enthusiastic support of this project and for Cart for a Cause. They have brought much to us and we are honored to have them as a partner in our mission to feed those in need.

We would also like to thank our media partner *Food & Wine Magazine* for their support.

POM Wonderful and FIJI Water have been with us from the beginning of Cart for a Cause and this project, offering their support, recipes, and ideas.

But most of all, we would like to thank Sister Alice Marie Quinn, founder and director of St. Vincent Meals on Wheels, for being such a constant spirit and advocate for those who are in need of a meal. Without her none of this would have been possible.

November 2011

Dear Epicurean Enthusiasts,

Every great meal has three primary ingredients: preparation, passion and perseverance.

Whether a famous chef is creating a five-course meal, a parent is cooking for a family celebration, or people are volunteering their time to make and deliver Meals on Wheels, preparation, passion and perseverance play a vital role.

Lexus is proud to recognize the efforts of the many people who have brought you the "Cart for a Cause" cookbook. We also celebrate all of you who have purchased this cookbook and hope that these recipes lead to fabulous meals for you, your family and your friends.

But most importantly, your contribution will benefit St. Vincent Meals on Wheels program, which brings meals and companionship to people in need.

So whether you're creating a simple appetizer or the most elaborate dessert, don't forget to prepare, infuse your passion and always persevere. The result is guaranteed to be a success.

Enjoy your food and wine,

David Nordstrom
Vice President, Lexus Marketing

cart for a cause

The Junior Advisory Board of St. Vincent Meals on Wheels in 2010 launched CART FOR A CAUSE (CFAC), Los Angeles' first and only fully philanthropic lunch truck.

Cart for a Cause has hosted restaurants such as Nobu West Hollywood, Comme Ça, Animal, STREET, The Foundry, the Lazy Ox Canteen, Il Grano, Little Door, Church & State, The Gorbals, FIG, Asia de Cuba, Luques, Tavern, and AOC, among many others.

All net proceeds of the truck go directly to supporting St. Vincent Meals on Wheels, the largest privately funded chapter of Meals on Wheels of America. These funds are vital in helping this organization prepare, serve, and deliver over 4,700 meals every day.

Cart for a Cause provides:

Specially crafted lunches by L.A.'s best restaurants

Beverages and snacks from FIJI Water, POM Wonderful, and Wonderful Pistachios

Cookies from Miss Lilly's Trading Company

St. Vincent Meals on Wheels recognizes the tireless efforts of the Junior Advisory Board who have made Cart for a Cause possible:

Ed Choi	Terri Robison
Rick Llanos	Greg Sato
Andrei Najjar	Jennifer Sommer
Cater Reese	

st. vincent senior citizen nutrition program mission

The mission of the St. Vincent Senior Citizen Nutrition Program (AKA St. Vincent Meals on Wheels) is to prepare and deliver well-balanced, nutritious meals to homebound elderly and other vulnerable residents within a 43-square-mile target area of Los Angeles.

Equally important are the preventive goals of heading off the degenerative processes brought on by malnutrition and of enabling seniors and others to remain independent in their own homes for as long as possible.

Most program participants are too frail or too ill to shop for and prepare food, while others are disabled or suffering from debilitating disease. We are especially committed to meeting the needs of the indigent and partially indigent. The St. Vincent Senior Citizen Nutrition Program serves anyone in need, regardless of age, illness, disability, race, or religion.

This mission has not changed since the program's inception in 1977.

st. vincent meals on wheels facts

Since 1977, St. Vincent Meals on Wheels has prepared and delivered nourishing meals to homebound seniors and seriously ill adults across Los Angeles.

The largest privately funded meal program in the country, we provide a lifeline of healthful meals and daily home visits to more than 3,000 homebound seniors and seriously ill adults who cannot shop or cook for themselves.

Our meals are provided to any homebound person in need, regardless of religion, age, national origin, disability, illness, or ability to pay.

In 2010 alone, we served a total of 1,172,282 meals! A nutritious, home-delivered meal can help to:

Keep seniors independent and out of nursing homes

Give those who are ill the energy to improve

Restore strength to the malnourished

Ease the pain of loneliness and isolation

Provide a way to make sure shut-ins are OK and offer assistance if they are not

Currently we serve an average of 4,700 meals per day to more than 2,700 clients across Los Angeles. In addition to a hot midday meal, some clients also receive a cold supper. Those who depend on us for everything they eat also receive breakfast.

Donations of $2.50 per meal are asked but not required. Clients—many on fixed incomes—are asked to pay what they can afford. The cost of each meal is $6.98.

To deliver meals to our clients, we drive about 620 miles a day. Our fleet of 36 delivery cars and vans is donated.

With a paid staff of 98, we rely on more than 275 volunteers to help prepare and deliver meals seven days a week.

St. Vincent Meals on Wheels depends on your private charitable support, not the government, to fulfill our mission. For more information, call Sister Alice Marie Quinn, founder and executive director, at (213) 484-7778.

Thank you for delivering food and love to L.A.'s hungry seniors!

PRESENTED BY LEXUS

sister alice marie quinn, d.c.

Sister Alice Marie Quinn, Daughter of Charity and registered dietitian, is the founder and program director of St. Vincent Meals on Wheels. Under her leadership, St. Vincent Meals on Wheels has become the largest privately funded Meals on Wheels program in America.

Today St. Vincent Meals on Wheels prepares and delivers more than 4,700 meals each day, which includes hot meals, cold meals, frozen meals, and weekly breakfast deliveries, across Los Angeles.

Sister infuses St. Vincent Meals on Wheels with a spirit of generosity through her compassion, leadership, and wisdom.

"In the beginning, it was just us and a few pots of stew. But the response was tremendous, and it became impossible to ignore the great need in the community. Over the years it became so much more than plates of food; it became friendship, family, and nourishment for the soul."

—Sister Alice Marie

eggplant bake

MAKES 40 SERVINGS

Cooking spray
14 eggs, slightly beaten
6 cups seasoned dry bread crumbs
6 eggplants, sliced into ½-inch rounds
2 6-pound cans marinara sauce
6 cups grated mozzarella cheese
1½ cups grated Parmesan cheese, or more
    if desired

Preheat the oven to 350°F.

Spray four 9 × 13-inch baking dishes or other large baking pans with cooking spray.

Place the eggs and crumbs in separate bowls. Dip the eggplant slices in the eggs, then in bread crumbs.

Put the eggplant on baking sheets in a single layer and bake for 15 minutes.

In the prepared baking dishes, layer the eggplant, mozzarella, and marinara sauce, and sprinkle with some of the Parmesan cheese. Repeat layers to thickness desired. Sprinkle Parmesan cheese generously on the top layer.

Bake for 30 minutes, until the cheese is melted and bubbly. Let sit for about 10 minutes before serving.

jose hernandez

Jose came to Meals on Wheels through the Summer Youth Program in 1996, when he was just fifteen. After two months, he was hired to deliver meals on weekends. After attending one semester of college, he returned to work full-time at Meals on Wheels. In 2003, Jose entered Trade Tech Culinary School. When not in school, he continued to work part-time and assist the cooks. Over the years we hired several other employees with the same name—Jose Hernandez. So it was necessary to give them each a number; our "baby chef" became Jose #1, and he has carried the name very well.

After graduation in June 2005, he became a part of our "Culinary Team." He is creative, has a natural passion for food, and is always trying to improve the flavors of our many special diets with fresh herbs and seasonings. We have a six-week cycle menu and Jose says that "even with the cycle menu, there is always something different to create and cook differently." Jose Hernandez proudly lives up to his name, Jose #1.

octavio becerra

Octavio Becerra is chef and principal of palate food + wine. Born and raised in Los Angeles, Octavio grew up in the restaurant industry. His long stint with Joachim Splichal as cofounder of the Patina Group paved the way for his most recent opening, palate food +wine, in Glendale, California. Irene Virbila of the Los Angeles Times *proclaimed palate "the most exciting and delicious new restaurant to open in a very long time." palate food + wine is a wine-centric restaurant with a wine bar and wine store on the premises, focusing on the natural relationship between food and wine. This is realized through the thoughtful selection and preparation of the unique ingredients and attributes of the palette, allowing the guest to create and enjoy pairings for the mind, mouth, and memories.*

Chocolate Pudding

1½ cups sugar

¾ cup cocoa powder

½ cup cornstarch

⅛ teaspoon kosher salt

4 cups whole milk

2 cups half-and-half

3 ounces Valrhona bittersweet chocolate, chopped

1 tablespoon vanilla extract

3 ounces white chocolate, chopped

Crème fraîche, for topping

Macerated Strawberries

1 pint strawberries, thinly sliced

¼ cup granulated sugar

1½ teaspoons fresh lemon juice

chocolate pudding and macerated strawberries

MAKES 6 SERVINGS

Make the Chocolate Pudding: Whisk together the first four ingredients in a mixing bowl. Slowly add the milk, whisking until smooth. Slowly add the half-and-half, whisking until smooth.

Pour the mixture through a fine sieve into a saucepan. Bring to a boil over medium heat, whisking continuously. Simmer gently for 2 minutes.

Turn off the heat and stir in the Valrhona chocolate, vanilla extract, and white chocolate.

Transfer the pudding to a mixing bowl. Fill a larger mixing bowl with ice cubes. Rest the bowl with the pudding on top of the ice and let the mixture cool (about 15 minutes) while stirring frequently.

Pour the mixture into 1-cup ramekins, cups, or mugs. Refrigerate until well chilled.

Make the Macerated Strawberries: Place the sliced strawberries in a nonreactive bowl. Stir in the sugar and lemon juice. Let sit for about 20 minutes or until the strawberries release their juices.

Serve each pudding with a few strawberries and a bit of whipped crème fraîche.

alex q. becker

Alex Quint Becker, executive chef at Nobu West Hollywood, brings years of experience and a creative talent to the famed Nobu empire. Night after night, Becker and his highly trained staff continue to uphold the solid reputation of Nobu Matsuhisa's world-renowned cuisine. Furthermore, he has put his own twists on Nobu's Peruvian-influenced fare, creating local dishes such as Wagyu Tacos, Foie Gras Crispy Soba, and Avocado-Crusted Sea Bass, which have developed a loyal following, leaving Angelenos craving for more.

Prior to his current position at Nobu West Hollywood, Becker spent two years at Nobu 57 in New York. Becker proved himself an innovative chef and in 2007 went on to open the Waikiki Nobu location as sous chef. Before becoming a part of the Nobu family, Becker spent time mastering his craft in Caluso, Italy, where he studied at the Italian Culinary Institute for Foreigners, worked at Michelin-starred Ristorante Gardenia di Caluso, and, most importantly, submerged himself in the rich Italian culture.

Becker's refined training combined with his creativity, passion, and adventurous nature make him an obvious success at Nobu West Hollywood, where diners from around the world gather to experience world-renowned cuisine.

ribeye with almond nori kaba rub

Make the Nori Rub: Toast the nori sheets until they reach a nice golden brown. They will shrink. Hand-crumble the nori into a bowl.

Put the coriander, cumin, salt, and cayenne in a spice grinder. Blend until fine. Add the crumbled nori and pulse to blend.

Transfer to a bowl and add the rest of the ingredients. Mix well.

Make the Almond Rosemary Cream: In a blender, combine all ingredients except for the mayonnaise and blend well. Let rest for 10 minutes, strain, then add this liquid to the mayonnaise and mix well.

Cook the Ribeye: Heat a grill to high. Rub the steak with the nori rub. Place on the hot grill. Cook both sides until the meat reaches the desired temperature. Serve the steak with an herb salad and the almond cream.

Nori Rub

10 nori sheets

1¼ teaspoons coriander

½ teaspoon ground cumin

1 teaspoon Maldon sea salt

¼ teaspoon cayenne

1½ teaspoons minced garlic

1⅔ teaspoons ginger oroshi

3 tablespoons plus 1 teaspoon extra-virgin olive oil

2 teaspoons almond oil

½ cup Original Oven Roasted Almond Accents® (crushed)

1½ tablespoons almond flour

Almond Rosemary Cream

1 tablespoon plus 2 teaspoons lemon juice

1 tablespoon plus 2 teaspoons usukuchi soy

3 tablespoons rosemary leaves

1 tablespoon almond oil

½ cup mayonnaise

Six 6-ounce portions of ribeye

jeremy berlin

Jeremy Berlin attended a community college culinary program and landed his first job cooking at L'Auberge in Dayton, Ohio. Berlin then decided to head east and study at the French Culinary Institute in New York City, where he also went on to work with some of this country's top French chefs, such as Philippe Bertineau at Payard Patisserie & Bistro, Eric Ripert at the three-Michelin-starred Le Bernardin, and Cyril Renaud at Fleur de Sel. Jeremy most recently worked under renowned chef Gordon Ramsay at Gordon Ramsay at the London NYC, and then he came out west to open Gordon Ramsay at the London West Hollywood. Currently, Jeremy heads the kitchen at Church & State.

vegetable bayaldi

MAKES 4 TO 6 SERVINGS

Preheat the oven to 350°F.

Slice the onion and sauté in a little olive oil in a pan until it turns a rich golden brown. Set aside.

Thinly slice the zucchini, eggplants, and tomatoes.

Place the cooked onion on the bottom of an 8-inch square baking pan and layer the vegetables one after the other on top of the onion.

Season with salt and pepper, then pour the ¼ cup olive oil on top.

Cover with parchment paper and bake for 45 minutes to 1 hour, until the vegetables are fully cooked and tender.

Remove from the oven and let cool. Serve at room temperature. Can be served on bread.

1 yellow onion
¼ cup olive oil, plus more for cooking the onion
1 yellow zucchini or other yellow squash
1 green zucchini
2 Japanese eggplants
6 ripe Roma tomatoes
Kosher salt and ground black pepper, to taste
Bread (optional, for serving)

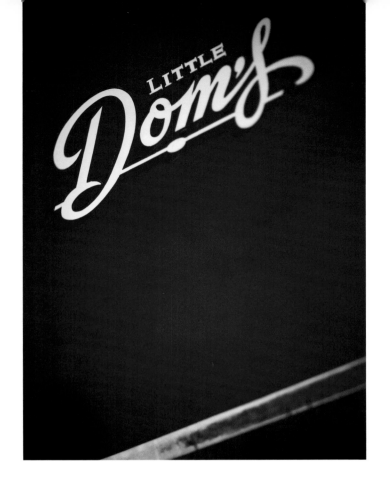

brandon
boudet

Brandon Boudet, co-owner and executive chef of Dominick's, Little Dom's, and the 101 Coffee Shop, brings his love of Italian-American cuisine to the streets of Los Angeles. He was born and raised in New Orleans, where his family celebrated life with generous portions of Louisiana and Italian cooking. Although Boudet has worked for luminaries such as Paul Prudhomme and Emeril Lagasse, he ranks his two grandmothers, one a talented Louisiana home chef, the other a master of Italian cuisine, as his greatest influences. Boudet's culinary philosophy is reflected in his approachable yet urbane menus, where he puts his own signature twist on Italian-American classics like spaghetti and meatballs, panini, house-made pastas, and wood-oven pizzas.

spaghetti and meatballs

Make the Soffritto: Finely chop all ingredients. Set aside for use in both the meatballs and sauce.

Make the Meatballs: Preheat the oven to 375°F.

Heat the olive oil in a sauté pan over medium heat. Add 1½ cups of the soffritto and sauté for about 3 minutes.

Combine the soffritto and all remaining ingredients in a large bowl and mix well. Using a 2½-ounce ice cream scoop, scoop the meat mixture into balls. Bake on a sheet pan lined with parchment paper for 15 minutes .

Make the Tomato Sauce: Heat the olive oil in a large pot. Add 4 cups of the soffritto and sauté for 3 minutes. Add the salt, sugar, pepper flakes, and tomato paste and sauté for 2 minutes. Add the tomatoes and simmer for 3 hours. Remove from heat, add the basil and oregano, and leave in the sauce until completely cooled to infuse flavor.

Assemble the Dish: Remove the cheesecloth-wrapped herbs and discard. Reheat the tomato sauce and serve with the meatballs over cooked spaghetti.

Soffritto
(makes 5½ cups, enough for meatballs and sauce)

4 celery ribs
2 large yellow onions
15 garlic cloves
1 bunch fresh flat-leaf parsley

Dominick's Meatballs

¼ cup olive oil
1½ cups of the soffritto
2½ pounds ground pork
2½ pounds ground beef
1 tablespoon ground fennel seeds
1 teaspoon red pepper flakes
1 tablespoon porcini mushroom powder
1 cup sliced mushrooms, sautéed for
    5 minutes
4 cups dry bread crumbs
2 eggs
1 tablespoon salt

Dominick's Tomato Sauce

¼ cup olive oil
4 cups of the soffritto
1 tablespoon salt
1 teaspoon sugar
1 teaspoon red pepper flakes
3 tablespoons tomato paste
6 28-ounce cans of tomatoes, passed
    through a food mill
1 bunch each of basil and oregano, wrapped
    in cheesecloth

josef centeno

Josef Centeno is the chef/partner at Lazy Ox Canteen. His approach to cuisine enlarges upon a rigorous training blended with a diverse ethnic heritage. Josef has been nurturing diners for the last fourteen years, beginning his career at Daniel, La Cote Basque, and Les Celebrites in New York. He was executive chef at Meson G and Opus in Los Angeles. His culinary ingredient-driven inventiveness draws on inspiration from modern and traditional French, Mexican, Japanese, and Catalan cuisines.

lace-battered white anchovies with saffron honey water

MAKES 12 SERVINGS

Make the Lace Batter: Combine the flour and cornstarch and whisk in the liquid. Add more liquid if needed to achieve a light batter consistency. Refrigerate until ready to use.

Make the Honey Water: Combine saffron and water and let steep for 10 minutes. Mix in the honey until dissolved.

Cook the Anchovies: In a stockpot, heat the oil to 375°F.

Lightly dust the fish in flour, then dip in batter. Shake off the excess and gently swirl in the hot oil.

Fry for about 1 minute or until golden brown. Remove and drain on paper towels.

Place on a serving plate and drizzle with honey water.

Lace Batter

1 cup all-purpose flour
½ cup cornstarch
2 cups sparkling water or beer, or
    more if needed

Honey Water

7 threads saffron
2 tablespoons warm water
½ cup honey

Anchovies

1 dozen fresh white anchovies
    or smelts
Flour for dusting
1 quart peanut oil

onil chibás

Onil Chibás grew up in New York City. While studying music at Boston University, Onil worked at several hotels and fine dining restaurants throughout Boston. The culmination of this work led to his selection on the opening team of Chef Lydia Shire's highly successful restaurant, Biba.

In 1991, Onil moved to Los Angeles to follow another dream: being a filmmaker. He worked for more than a decade in animation with Disney Feature Animation, Sony Pictures, and DreamWorks Feature Animation.

In 2003, Onil left the entertainment industry to pursue his lifelong passion of food. Graduating top of his class from the California School of Culinary Arts, Onil accepted an externship at Joachim Splichal's flagship restaurant, Patina (at the Walt Disney Concert Hall). Upon completion, Onil went on to launch The Elements Food Group—now comprising a full-service catering division along with the acclaimed Pasadena restaurants Elements Café and Elements Kitchen.

marinated flank steak with kimchi tacos

MAKES 16 SMALL TACOS

Kimchi

2 heads napa cabbage

½ cup kosher salt

3 tablespoons chopped garlic

3 tablespoons chopped fresh ginger

1 cup julienned carrots

½ cup sliced scallions, green part only,
    cut on the bias

2 tablespoons fish sauce (nam pla)

3 tablespoons toasted black sesame seeds

Sambal chili sauce to taste (found in most
    Asian markets)

Sesame oil to taste

Granulated sugar to taste

Sriracha chili sauce to taste

Rice wine vinegar to taste

Pickled Ginger

1 pound fresh ginger, peeled and sliced
    paper-thin (a mandoline is helpful with this)

½ cup kosher salt

1 cup rice vinegar

½ cup granulated sugar

Corn and Sesame Tortillas

2 cups maseca (white corn paste)

1½ cups water

1 tablespoon sesame oil

2 tablespoons toasted black sesame seeds

Salt and pepper to taste

Sambal Aïoli

5 garlic cloves, finely minced

1 cup prepared or homemade mayonnaise

Sambal chili sauce to taste

Salt and pepper to taste

Juice of 1 lemon

Steak

¾ cup soy sauce

1½ tablespoons grated fresh ginger

1½ tablespoons hoisin sauce

1 stalk lemongrass, tenderized and minced

3 tablespoons sesame oil

¼ cup rice wine vinegar

1 bunch scallions, minced, plus 1 small bunch
    scallions, green part only, cut on the bias

4 garlic cloves, minced

1½ pounds flank steak, trimmed and left whole

Canola oil, for grilling

Make the Kimchi: Roughly chop the cabbage into bite-size pieces, place in a large bowl, and cover with the ½ cup kosher salt. Let sit for 3 hours, then rinse really well. After this process, mix all the remaining ingredients together with the cabbage and store in a covered plastic container in the refrigerator.

Make the Pickled Ginger: Mix the ginger slices with the ½ cup of salt and let sit for 1 hour. Then rinse

the ginger thoroughly in cold water until all the salt has been removed. Heat the vinegar and sugar together until the sugar dissolves, then pour over the ginger. Cover and let cool to room temperature. Store in the refrigerator.

Make the Tortillas: Mix all ingredients in a bowl until blended. Take a 1-gallon zip-top bag and cut down either side, leaving the bottom intact. Lightly spray with nonstick spray. Shape the tortilla batter into 1½- to 2-ounce balls. Place each tortilla ball between the 2 sides of the bag and press with the bottom of a sauté pan to about ⅛ inch thick. (Or you can use a tortilla press.) Cook in a nonstick pan without oil for 30 seconds on each side. Set aside.

Make the Sambal Aïoli: In a bowl, mix together the garlic and mayonnaise. Add sambal to desired spiciness. Season with salt and pepper. Add a squeeze of lemon for balance and brightness.

Prepare the Steak: Place all ingredients except the steak and the small bunch of bias-cut scallions in a bowl and whisk together. Place the steak in a dish and pour the marinade over the meat to cover completely. Let marinate overnight in the refrigerator.

Remove from the marinade. Heat the grill to smoking and season the grill with canola oil. Sear the steak on all sides, being careful to not overcook. Remove from the grill and let sit for 20 to 30 minutes.

When ready to serve, slice the steak into bite-size strips and reheat in a frying pan just until hot.

Assemble the Dish: Reheat the tortillas in a nonstick pan. Place 2 or 3 pieces of hot steak on each tortilla, top with kimchi, pickled ginger, and sambal aïoli, and garnish with the bias-cut scallions.

Chef Michael DeMaria, chef/owner of M Catering by Michael's and Heirloom: An American Restaurant, is renowned throughout the Phoenix Metropolitan region and beyond for his inventive and exceptional American and Italian contemporary cuisines. Chef Michael was trained by the superior chefs at the five-star Arizona Biltmore. His dynamic background includes teaching culinary arts at the California Culinary Academy in San Francisco and working at well-known destinations such as San Francisco's Ritz-Carlton, Phoenix's famous Royal Palms Hotel and Lon's at the Hermosa Inn, the Wilshire Country Club in Los Angeles, and Westin Hotel Corporation. In 1992, Chef Michael was selected as one of twenty-five chefs to comprise Team U.S.A., which represented the United States in the Culinary Olympics in Frankfurt, Germany. For a decade, 1997–2009, Chef Michael's highly acclaimed namesake restaurant, Michael's at the Citadel, located in the high Sonoran Desert of North Scottsdale, received recognitions such as the AAA 4-Diamond award, Mobil 3-Star award, Wine Spectator magazine's Award of Excellence, and the Zagat Survey's "extraordinary."

michael
demaria

shrimp meatballs with spicy puttanesca sauce

MAKES 6–8 SERVINGS

Make the Shrimp Meatballs: Pat the shrimp with paper towels to dry thoroughly. Place the shrimp in a food processor with the eggs and cream. Pulse until the mixture is smooth and chunky, but not pureed. In a bowl, combine the shrimp mix, parsley, chives, garlic, salt, and pepper.

Make the Poaching Liquid: Pour the clam juice, lemon juice, wine, peppercorns, and salt into a large stockpot. Bring to a boil, then turn down below a simmer to roughly 190° to poach.

Cook the Meatballs: Using a small ice cream scoop, drop the shrimp mixture into the poaching liquid in small batches, 5 to 7 balls at a time. When they float, remove them with a skimmer and put on a pan to cool.

Make the Puttanesca Sauce: Heat your favorite marinara sauce with the capers, anchovies, olives, and red pepper flakes. Simmer for approximately 20 minutes.

Assemble the Dish: Drop the pasta into a large pot of boiling salted water. While the pasta is cooking, heat the olive oil in a large sauté pan. Sear the shrimp meatballs, continuously rolling them around the pan to brown all sides. When browned, add a little lemon juice and your puttanesca sauce to the pan.

Strain the pasta and add it into the pan with the shrimp meatballs. Season with salt and pepper, stir, and serve.

Shrimp Meatballs

2 pounds shrimp, deveined, tail and
 shell removed
2 eggs
⅓ cup heavy cream
1 bunch flat-leaf Italian parsley (stems
 discarded), finely minced
1 bunch chives, thinly sliced
2 tablespoons minced roasted garlic
Salt and pepper to taste

Poaching Liquid

1½ quarts clam juice
2 cups lemon juice
1 cup white wine
½ cup black peppercorns
Salt to taste

Puttanesca Sauce

2 quarts your favorite marinara sauce
½ cup chopped capers
10 anchovy fillets, chopped fine
½ cup kalamata olives, chopped fine
1 tablespoon red pepper flakes

1 pound your favorite pasta
3–4 tablespoons olive oil (enough to coat
 the bottom of the pan)
Lemon juice to taste
Salt and pepper to taste

Whist executive chef Tony DiSalvo has created a fresh and vibrant menu combining inspiration from the Mediterranean coast with Santa Monica's best locally sourced fresh produce. After graduating from the Culinary Institute of America (CIA) in 1995, DiSalvo worked for a year with Philippe Schmidt at La Goulue, where he had his first experience with French Mediterranean cuisine. Next, he lent his skills to the kitchen of Gramercy Tavern under Tom Colicchio. In 1998, DiSalvo started at Jean Georges, the Michelin three-star restaurant in the Trump International Hotel and Tower in New York, and in 2001 became the famed restaurant's executive chef at the tender age of twenty-six. In 2004, DiSalvo left the East Coast and headed for Southern California, where he opened Jack's La Jolla as executive chef and led it to win four Mobil stars, among other accolades, before joining Whist in late 2009.

tony disalvo

disalvo family meatball recipe

MAKES ABOUT 40 MEATBALLS

Meatballs

2 pounds ground pork

2 pounds ground veal (see Note)

8 ounces ground pancetta

8 ounces ricotta cheese

8 ounces ciabatta, diced

12 ounces whole milk

5 eggs

Salt and ground pepper to taste

1 bunch flat-leaf parsley, coarsely chopped

Sauce

4 ounces olive oil

1 onion, diced

4 garlic cloves, chopped

2 28-ounce cans whole tomatoes, crushed

6 basil leaves, chopped

4 ounces Parmesan cheese, shaved

Make the Meatballs: In a bowl, combine the pork, veal, and pancetta. In another bowl, combine the ricotta, bread crumbs, milk, eggs, salt, and pepper. Mix well and allow to sit until the milk is fully absorbed.

Preheat the oven to 400°F.

Fold the bread mixture into the meat and add the parsley. Shape into 2-ounce balls and lay out on a parchment-lined sheet pan with an inch of space between each meatball. Bake for 15 minutes or until golden brown.

Make the Sauce: In a large saucepot, heat the olive oil and cook the onion and garlic until golden. Add the tomatoes and meatballs and simmer for 2 hours.

Finish with basil leaves and shaved Parmesan cheese.

Note: Ground beef can be substituted for the ground veal.

philip dubose

Philip DuBose, executive chef of Asia de Cuba at Mondrian L.A., graces the Los Angeles institution with more than twenty years of versatile experience from an impressive roster of world-class properties. One of DuBose's many culinary fortes is Asian-Latin fusion, as honed during his previous post with Asia de Cuba in San Francisco. With his skilled background, DuBose flawlessly executes the diverse and flavorful Asia de Cuba menu with ease while maintaining the unique sensibility that is the Mondrian L.A.

DuBose began his culinary career at 231 Ellsworth in San Mateo in 1990, followed by executive sous chef positions at many top-rated restaurants, such as Pacific'O in Maui (rated among Hawaii's Top Ten in the Zagat Survey); Los Angeles' Vida, Boxer, Five Feet, and Rock/Rockenwagner (one of the Top Ten Restaurants in Los Angeles, Gourmet 2000); and Whist at the Viceroy Santa Monica Hotel (voted one of the hottest hotels in the world by Condé Nast Traveler).

adc tuna pica

8 ounces Ahi tuna (sushi/sashimi-grade), finely diced
¼ cup sliced toasted almonds
1 tablespoon currants
1 tablespoon unsweetened shredded coconut
2 tablespoons finely minced Spanish olives,
1 teaspoon finely chopped fresh chives
2 ounces Pica Dressing
8 2-inch wonton squares, fried for a few seconds until crispy
4 ounces Cucumber Escabeche

Pica Dressing

2 ounces soy sauce
1 tablespoon minced fresh ginger
1 tablespoon lime juice
2 tablespoons water
½ teaspoon minced garlic
Pinch of Togarashi pepper
1 tablespoon chili oil

Cucumber Escabeche

5 ounces English cucumber
¼ red pepper, finely julienned
½ teaspoon Togarashi pepper
¼ cup rice wine vinegar
1 tablespoon honey

Make the Pica Dressing: Combine all ingredients in a bowl and mix well. Refrigerate until needed.

Make the Cucumber Escabeche: Thinly slice the cucumber (use a Japanese slicer or a mandoline). Combine the cucumber with the red pepper, Togarashi pepper, vinegar, and honey. Allow to marinate for approximately 2 hours.

Assemble the Tuna Pica: In a mixing bowl, combine the tuna, almonds, currants, coconut, olives, chives, and dressing. Once gently mixed, divide evenly among the wonton squares. Stack 4 wontons "Napoleon style"; repeat with the remaining wontons. Gently squeeze any excess liquid from the cucumbers. Place the Cucumber Escabeche in the middle of the plate and the wonton stacks of tuna on each side of the plate.

Happy cooking!

Susan Feniger is an award-winning American chef, restaurateur, cookbook author, and radio and TV personality considered to be a leading authority on Latin cuisine in the United States. Wherever you are in the world, you're on Susan Feniger's STREET. Susan has been exploring global flavors for over thirty years and joyfully bringing her passion, knowledge, experience, and great food to your table. Join her on the journey and discover secrets of true cooks from cultures all over the world. Share the common language of people everywhere—food. And let Susan Feniger be your guide!

susan feniger

Heat the butter over medium-high heat in a heavy pan until frothy. Add the marshmallows and lower the heat. Push and stir with a rubber spatula so they don't burn onto the bottom of the pan.

When the marshmallows are halfway melted, add all the remaining ingredients *except* the millet and stir well.

Remove from the heat, add the millet, and stir until all the millet is mixed and evenly coated in the spiced marshmallow mix. Pour into a bowl.

Immediately start rolling into very small, ⅛-ounce balls. If you dampen your hands slightly with cold water, the mixture will be easier to work with. Place the balls in a container, uncovered, until they dry out slightly, about 1 hour.

We love serving these in a paper cone or a brown paper bag. They also make a great gift to take to someone for a party.

Note: Curry leaf can be purchased at an Indian market.

millet puffs

MAKES 72 ⅛-OUNCE BALLS

1 ounce (2 tablespoons) unsalted butter
5 ounces marshmallows
1 tablespoon whole cumin seed
1 teaspoon whole fennel seed
1 teaspoon black mustard seed
¾ teaspoon chile powder (Reshampati or cayenne)
¼ teaspoon ground turmeric
2 ounces dried currants
½ teaspoon kosher salt
1 teaspoon chopped curry leaf (see Note)
3 cups puffed millet (Arrowhead Mills)

michael fiorelli

Michael Fiorelli is chef de cuisine of Southern California's hottest new dining establishment—mar'sel, located at Terranea Resort. Just twenty miles south of LAX and situated on an expansive 102 oceanfront acres, Terranea serves up spectacular views of the Pacific Ocean— with none better than those at its signature restaurant, mar'sel, which features Fiorelli's interpretations of a California-inspired menu. His colorful dishes, refreshing presentations, and strict attention to detail impress even the most sophisticated palate.

"My inspiration comes from farmers who dedicate their lives to respecting the earth and their local communities. A great dish starts with the freshest seasonal ingredients," says Fiorelli. When asked his favorite food, Fiorelli says it's salt. "My whole cooking philosophy stems from the idea that great food needs two things: love and salt."

eggplant cakes

MAKES 4 APPETIZER SERVINGS

1 large eggplant, halved lengthwise, flesh
    side scored
Olive oil, as needed
Salt and freshly ground black pepper
2 tablespoons finely diced yellow onion
2 tablespoons finely diced red bell pepper
2 tablespoons golden raisins
2 tablespoons pine nuts, toasted in a small,
    heavy-bottomed sauté pan
2 teaspoons each chopped fresh parsley,
    basil, oregano
2 tablespoons grated Parmigiano-Reggiano
2 pinches red pepper flakes
Flour, for dredging
Egg wash (made from 1 lightly beaten egg and
    ¼ cup cold water whisked together)
Canola oil, for pan-frying

Cook the Eggplant: Preheat the oven to 325°F. Coat the eggplant liberally on the scored side with olive oil and sprinkle with salt and pepper.

Lay the eggplant cut side up in a baking dish and roast until soft and golden brown, about 30 minutes, flipping over once.

Let cool. Scoop the eggplant flesh into a dishtowel (discarding the skin) and ring out excess water. Puree in the food processor and set aside.

Make the Cakes: Sauté the onion and bell pepper in some olive oil until very soft, fully cooked, and translucent. Two minutes before the peppers and onions are done cooking, add the raisins just to warm through and plump slightly. Allow to cool.

Add all ingredients to the eggplant, including 2 ounces of the bread crumbs. Season to taste with salt and pepper. Form patties by rolling balls to your desired size, then flattening slightly.

Dredge the patties in flour, then dip them in egg wash and coat them with extra bread crumbs. Pan-fry the patties in canola oil over medium heat until golden brown, about 30 minutes per side.

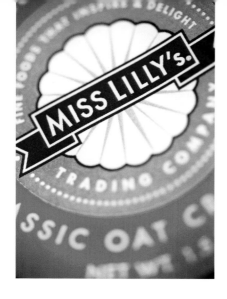

bebe flynn

Bebe Flynn, founder of Miss Lilly's Trading Company, has been baking cookies and brownies for as long as she can remember. Miss Lilly's represents Bebe's lifelong call to action. In 2009 Bebe founded Miss Lilly's Trading Company in order to help seniors and their pets by providing pet food to the home bound. The mission of Miss Lilly's Trading Company is to use a percentage of the profits from selling gourmet cookies to provide pet food to Meals on Wheels clients who own pets. Seeing her company come to fruition makes perfect sense: Bebe is a person who has a unique skill for combining her passions, philanthropy, and entrepreneurial prowess—and for making everyone she meets marvel at her energy and guffaw with laughter at her stories. She is wildly passionate about both helping the elderly and rescuing pets—and she makes a mean chocolate chip cookie.

Bebe is passionate about the difference Miss Lilly's can make to seniors and their pets. Miss Lilly herself is a King Charles Spaniel mix whom Bebe rescued and loves so much that she decided to name her dream company after her.

Miss Lilly's gourmet cookies can be purchased at Whole Foods, Bristol Farms, and online at www.misslillystradingcompany. com. Miss Lilly's elegant gift tins can be purchased exclusively at Saks 5th Avenue in Beverly Hills as well as online. A percentage of the profits directly benefits St. Vincent Meals on Wheels.

lilly's brownies

4 ounces (4 squares) 60%–65% cacao chocolate
¾ cup (1½ sticks) unsalted butter
1 cup granulated sugar
2 eggs
2 teaspoons vanilla
1 cup all-purpose flour

Preheat the oven to 350°F.
Grease an 8-inch square baking pan.

Melt the chocolate and butter in a saucepan over medium heat, stirring until melted. Transfer to a mixing bowl and, with an electric mixer on low speed, beat in the sugar. Beat in the eggs and vanilla, then stir in the flour.

Spread in the prepared pan and bake for 35 minutes.

lilly's cream cheese brownies

Heat 4 ounces cream cheese until creamy in the microwave (less than 1 minute) or on the stove in a double boiler. Spoon on top of the brownie mixture in the pan and swirl in lightly. Bake for 35 minutes.

ray garcia

A native Angeleno, Ray's passion for cuisine was cultivated while helping his grandmother prepare their weekly Sunday dinners. Though food remained an interest, he originally planned to pursue a legal career. Following graduation, he opted out of law school and instead enrolled at the California School of Culinary Arts. Prior to opening FIG Restaurant in Santa Monica in February 2009, Ray spent years perfecting his craft. He trained under renowned chefs, including Douglas Keene at Cyrus and Thomas Keller at the French Laundry, where he learned the importance of fresh seasonal ingredients.

warm quinoa salad with orange-blossom vinaigrette

MAKES 4 SERVINGS

Quinoa Salad

3½ ounces red quinoa

1 cup vegetable stock

1 sprig rosemary

Olive oil, for cooking

2 ounces butternut squash

½ Granny Smith apple, diced (peel if desired)

2 ounces Swiss chard stems and leaves, finely chopped

2 ounces haricots verts, blanched

1 ounce sliced almonds, toasted

Orange-Blossom Vinaigrette

1 cup orange juice

¼ cup orange-blossom honey

½ cup white balsamic vinegar

1 cup olive oil

Make the Vinaigrette: Reduce the orange juice by one-third. Allow to cool. When the orange juice has cooled, add the honey and vinegar and whisk in the olive oil. Set aside.

Make the Quinoa Salad: Preheat the oven to 350°F.

Combine the quinoa, vegetable stock, and rosemary in a medium saucepan, bring to a simmer, and cook until tender, about 15 minutes. When the quinoa is cooked, drain the liquid and toss with a little olive oil.

Peel and seed the butternut squash, cut into ½-inch cubes, toss with oil, place in a baking pan, and roast for 15 minutes or until fork-tender.

Heat a little olive oil in a medium sauté pan. Add the apples, Swiss chard, and blanched haricot verts and sauté until the apples are soft.

Mix the roasted squash and sautéed ingredients with the quinoa and dress with the vinaigrette. Garnish with toasted almond slices.

joseph gillard

Being raised on a forty-acre homestead in Fremont, Michigan, made a lasting impression on Gillard as to the integrity and beauty of local and seasonal food products. He joined Napa Valley Grille in 2007, where his appreciation for locally grown ingredients and strong relationships with California farmers helped him craft a culinary signature that was the perfect fit for the restaurant's wine country cuisine. Over the last four years, Gillard has infused Napa Valley Grille with a new perspective and philosophy, resulting in a reinvented restaurant that offers guests an exceptional, chef-driven fine dining experience that is approachable, value-oriented, and built around his commitment to connecting with guests. This can be seen through his weekly farmer's market walk-throughs and personal labor of love, the restaurant's nonprofit Community-Supported Agriculture (CSA) program. Outside of the kitchen, Gillard, a Sherman Oaks resident, regularly contributes his time to several Los Angeles fundraisers.

prime beef sirloin jerky

MAKES ABOUT 4 OUNCES DRIED JERKY

1 pound prime beef sirloin or flank steak
2 teaspoons smoked sea salt (see Note)
1 teaspoon onion powder
1 teaspoon garlic powder
1 ounce chipotle peppers in
adobo sauce, minced

Trim all the fat and silverskin from the meat and slice thinly with the grain. (To make slicing easier, freeze the beef for 30 minutes before slicing.) Place the beef in a nonreactive bowl.

Place all other ingredients in a spice grinder or coffee grinder used for this purpose. Process to a paste.

Add the paste to the beef and mix well, until the meat is thoroughly coated with the paste. Let marinate, covered, in the refrigerator for 24 hours.

Place the beef in a single layer on dehydrator racks or cooling racks, spaced evenly to ensure even drying. (A little space between the pieces allows the air to move freely around the beef.) Dry the beef until very dry (about 24 hours), checking every 4 hours. Store in an airtight container in the refrigerator for up to 2 weeks.

Note: Smoked sea salt varies by brand. It is important to find a brand that is actually smoked and not adulterated with liquid smoke. The salt is cold smoked on screens.

Suzanne Goin was raised by foodie parents in Los Angeles. While in high school and college, she worked at Ma Maison and L'Orangerie in L.A. and Al Forno in Providence, Rhode Island.

After two years at Chez Panisse, a year at two-star restaurants in Paris, and three years in Boston under Todd English and Jody Adams, she returned to work at Campanile as executive chef before opening Lucques in 1998. She now has three restaurants—opening AOC in 2002 and Tavern in 2009— and has won a James Beard award for Outstanding Chef in California as well as Outstanding Cookbook for Sunday Suppers at Lucques.

suzanne goin

3 tablespoons finely diced shallots
1 teaspoon lemon juice
¼ teaspoon salt, or to taste
1 tablespoon pomegranate molasses
¼ cup extra-virgin olive oil
½ cup POM Wonderful pomegranate arils
1 tablespoon chopped fresh flat-leaf parsley

pomegranate salsa

MAKES 1 CUP

Mix the shallots, lemon juice, and salt in a small bowl, and let sit 5 minutes. Whisk in the pomegranate molasses and then the olive oil. Stir in the pomegranate arils and the parsley. Taste for balance and seasoning.

mark gold

Eva Restaurant is named after Chef Mark Gold's grandmother. Born and raised in Brooklyn, New York, Grandma Eva became Mark Gold's cooking inspiration—combining personality, warmth, and care to prepare home-cooked meals using only what was available to her.

Eva Restaurant is now known to most guests as their home away from home. Chef Gold welcomes his guests into his warm and inviting restaurant to experience his contemporary American cuisine, which is simple, refined, seasonal, and enjoyable. The Eva menu changes frequently, as Chef Gold always cooks with what the season brings him. Eva also offers a hand-crafted artisan cocktail menu, boutique wine list, and special list of rotating craft beers so that Eva's guests always have plenty of options to experience each time they visit.

potato parmesan soup

1 yellow onion, sliced

1 fennel bulb, sliced

8 whole garlic cloves, peeled

1 Granny Smith apple, peeled and sliced

½ pound (2 sticks) unsalted butter

6 large Yukon gold potatoes, peeled
    and diced

1 gallon vegetable stock or chicken stock
    (see Note)

4 cups grated Parmigiano-Reggiano

1 cup heavy cream (optional)

Salt and white pepper to taste

1 lemon, juiced (about ¼ cup)

In a large stockpot, sauté the onion, fennel, garlic, and apple in the butter until translucent, about 15 minutes.

Add the potatoes and stock and bring to a boil, then simmer until the potatoes are fully cooked, about 30 minutes.

While the soup is still hot, puree in a blender in small batches. Stir in the cheese and the cream, if using. Puree in a blender in small batches. Season with salt, white pepper, and lemon juice.

Note: To make vegetable stock, in a soup pot combine 3 bunches leeks, roughly chopped; 2 cloves; 4 whole heads of garlic; and 1 bunch of parsley, roughly chopped. Cover with a gallon of water and simmer for 1 hour.

eric
greenspan

*Eric Greenspan is the owner and
chef of the Foundry on Melrose in
Hollywood. He has cooked in such
acclaimed restaurants as Alain
Ducasse, El Bulli, and Patina and
has been featured on* The Next Iron
Chef *and* Iron Chef America. *While
sophisticated in both preparation
and presentation, there is often a
touch of whimsy to Eric's cooking,
a style that can be summed up
only as "Modern American."*

Make the Tartare: Place the orange and carrot juices in a saucepan. Heat over medium high and cook until the juice is reduced to 1 ounce. Add all remaining ingredients and mix well.

Make the Carrot and Garlic Salad: Place the garlic in a small saucepan of cold water. Bring to a boil, then strain. Repeat 2 more times, then fry the garlic in a small amount of oil until lightly browned. In a small bowl, mix the garlic with the carrots and pomegranate seeds.

Make the Ponzu: Mix all ingredients.

Make the Carrot Puree: Simmer the carrot in the juice until soft, then place the carrot and juice in a blender. Blend until smooth.

Assemble the Dish: Liberally drizzle the pomegranate ponzu on a salad plate.

Place the albacore tartare on the drizzle. Arrange the carrot and garlic salad on top of the tartare. Drizzle the carrot puree on top of the salad.

albacore tartare with carrots, garlic, and pomegranate

MAKES 1 SERVING

Tartare

6 ounces carrot juice

6 ounces orange juice

1 ounce extra-virgin olive oil, infused with garlic

4 ounces sashimi-grade Monterey albacore, chopped into a near paste

Salt and pepper to taste

Carrot and Garlic Salad

1 garlic clove, thinly sliced

Olive oil, for frying

1 baby yellow carrot, shaved on a Japanese mandoline

1 baby red carrot, shaved on a Japanese mandoline

10 to 15 pomegranate seeds

Pomegranate Ponzu

6 ounces pomegranate juice, cooked and reduced to ½ ounce

½ ounce soy sauce

½ ounce garlic oil

Carrot Puree

1 large carrot, peeled and diced

4 ounces carrot juice

tim guiltinan

Chef Tim Guiltinan recalls watching his favorite cooking shows, Yan Can Cook *and Jeff Smith's* The Frugal Gourmet, *while in junior high school. His "aha" moment about a career as a chef happened when he was twenty-two years old.*

He sees restaurants as a combination of living art and theater: "Like a painter, a chef starts with a blank canvas," he says. "The four walls of the kitchen and dining room are that canvas; the equipment and staff are the brushes. It's theater every night. And like theater, a meal has a beginning, middle, and an end."

Guiltinan is currently executive chef at the historic Raymond Restaurant, where he continues to evolve as a chef. He has intelligently transitioned a classic American menu to modern, contemporary American cuisine. He focuses on using premium, fresh, and seasonal ingredients and incorporates various classic and modern cooking techniques to create a style that is uniquely his own.

green grape and almond gazpacho

Gazpacho

2 pounds sweet green grapes, stems removed

2 pounds cucumbers, peeled and chopped

1 cup toasted whole almond

½ cup extra-virgin olive oil

½ cup champagne vinegar

4 ounces crème fraiche (or sour cream)

4 large mint leaves

1 teaspoon salt

½ teaspoon freshly ground black pepper

Garnishes and Seasoning

Grape halves

Croutons

Espelette pepper to taste

Extra-virgin olive oil, for drizzling

Puree the soup ingredients in a blender until completely smooth. Strain through a medium-hole strainer. Garnish and season each soup as desired.

ilan hall

Born to travel-hungry Scottish and Israeli parents of Eastern European descent, Chef Ilan Hall was exposed to international food from an early age. At seventeen, Ilan began his journey in the culinary world, ultimately working for the likes of Tom Colicchio and Mario Batali. At twenty-four, Ilan's restless nature and tradition-shattering style earned him first place on Bravo TV's reality competition, Top Chef. *Today, Ilan can be found cooking in the open kitchen of his indefinable first restaurant—The Gorbals Los Angeles.*

bacon-wrapped matzo balls

MAKES ABOUT 125 BALLS

5 cups matzo meal
1½ tablespoons baking powder
18 large eggs
¾ cup melted pork lard or bacon fat
¾ cup FIJI Water
60–65 slices bacon, thinly sliced and cut in half
Horseradish sauce, for serving

In a large bowl, combine the matzo meal and baking powder. In a food processor, beat the eggs. While the eggs are beating, stream in the lard and FIJI Water. Pour into the matzo meal and baking powder and beat with a large whisk until incorporated, mixing well to avoid lumps. Let sit in the refrigerator for 1 hour.

Bring a large pot of well-salted water to a boil. Scoop cherry-size balls from the mixture. With moistened palms, roll them and drop into simmering water; cover and cook for about 30 minutes. The matzo balls will double in size. Remove and let cool.

While the balls are cooling, preheat the oven to 400°F.

Once cool to the touch, wrap each ball in half a slice of thin bacon and place on a perforated pan or rack (be sure the balls cannot fall through) set on a rimmed baking sheet. Make sure that the seam of the bacon is on the bottom of your ball so the bacon does not come loose while baking.

Bake the balls for about 20 minutes, or until the bacon is nice and crispy. Serve with horseradish sauce.

ashley james

For over twenty-five years, Chef Ashley James has aspired to create dishes that excite the five senses. As executive chef of Four Seasons Hotel Los Angeles, L.A.'s premier entertainment hangout, James has cooked for the A-list of Hollywood. With help from his team of global artisans, James's cuisine is based on classic French techniques and refined by a Mediterranean/California approach using locally sourced ingredients. Prior to arriving in Los Angeles, James was executive chef at the Four Seasons in Buenos Aires, where Le Mistral was awarded Best Restaurant in Argentina. Prior to joining Four Seasons Hotels and Resorts, James worked for ten years at highly acclaimed, Michelin-starred restaurants in Bordeaux, Paris, Mallorca (Spain), and England. James was named Young Chef of the Year in France and is a member of the L'Academie Culinaire Française.

POM velvet cupcakes with POM cream cheese frosting

MAKES 30 REGULAR CUPCAKES

POM Cream Cheese Frosting

Juice from 3 to 4 large POM Wonderful
  pomegranates (see Note), or 1½ cups POM
  Wonderful 100% pomegranate juice
1 cup arils from 1 to 2 large POM Wonderful
  pomegranates
4 ounces (1 stick) unsalted butter, softened
8 ounces cream cheese, at room temperature
14 ounces confectioners' sugar

POM Velvet Cupcakes

Juice from 6 to 9 large POM Wonderful
  pomegranates (see Note), or 2½ cups POM
  Wonderful 100% pomegranate juice
1 pound granulated sugar
14 ounces (3½ sticks) unsalted butter, softened
4 large eggs
1½ cups buttermilk
2 tablespoons white vinegar
2 teaspoons vanilla extract
15 ounces all-purpose flour
1½ ounces cocoa powder
4 teaspoons baking soda
Pinch of salt
¼ cup heavy cream

Make the Frosting: If not using bottled juice, prepare fresh pomegranate juice (see Note). Reduce the pomegranate juice, over low heat, down to 3 fluid ounces (about 6 tablespoons). Allow to cool.

Score 1 or 2 fresh pomegranates and place in a bowl of water. Break open the pomegranates under water to free the arils (seed sacs). The arils will sink to the bottom of the bowl and the membrane will float to the top. Sieve and put the arils in a separate bowl. Reserve 1 cup of the arils from the fruit and set aside. (Refrigerate or freeze the remaining arils for another use.)

Place the butter in the bowl of an electric mixer fitted with the paddle attachment and cream on medium-high speed for 1 minute.

Add the cream cheese and continue to mix for 2 more minutes.

Turn the speed down to low and slowly add the confectioners' sugar and the pomegranate juice reduction. Mix until the sugar is fully combined.

Remove the icing from the mixer and place in a piping bag with a round or star tip.

Make the Cupcakes: Preheat the oven to 350°F.

Reduce the pomegranate juice, over low heat, down to ½ cup.

Place the sugar and butter in the bowl of an electric mixer fitted with the paddle attachment. Cream on medium-high speed until the mixture is pale yellow and fluffy.

Turn the speed down to low and add the eggs one at a time.

In a separate bowl, combine the buttermilk, pomegranate juice reduction, white vinegar, and vanilla extract; slowly add half of this to the mixer bowl.

Combine the flour, cocoa powder, baking soda, and salt, and sift at least two times until well mixed. Add half of this to the mixer bowl.

Add the remaining half of the liquids to the mixer bowl, then the remaining dry ingredients. Finish off with the heavy cream. Beat just until combined.

Place cupcake liners in a cupcake pan and, using a spoon, fill with cake batter until just about three-quarters full.

Bake for 20 to 25 minutes, or until a toothpick inserted in the middle comes out clean.

Allow the pan to cool slightly, then transfer the cupcakes to a wire rack to cool completely. Once cool, they can be iced with the frosting and topped with fresh pomegranate arils.

Note: For 4 cups juice, cut 8 to 12 large POM Wonderful pomegranates in half and juice them with a citrus reamer or juicer. Pour the mixture through a cheesecloth-lined strainer or sieve. Set the juice aside.

david lentz

David Lentz was born and raised in Maryland. From a young age he developed a fondness for the sea and, more specifically, seafood. David began cooking professionally at the age of twenty and moved to Los Angeles in 2000 with the intention of owning and operating his own restaurant. After working with Mark Peel at Campanile, David opened the restaurants Firefly and Opaline.

In 2005, David opened the Hungry Cat in Hollywood to critical acclaim, the perfect jewel of a restaurant where casual food is raised to the level of an art form.

In 2007, David opened a second Hungry Cat location in Santa Barbara that showcases the freshest produce and seafood that the area has to offer.

crab cakes

MAKES 6 SERVINGS

1 pound Dungeness crabmeat

1 egg

1½ tablespoons Dijon mustard

1 tablespoon Worcestershire sauce

½ cup aïoli

1 cup crushed unsalted saltine crackers

Dash of Tabasco

Lemon juice to taste

Salt and pepper to taste

⅓ cup oil, for sautéing

Basic Aïoli

1 cup lemon juice

2 tablespoons water

2 tablespoons chopped fresh garlic

2 cups mayonnaise

2 tablespoons chopped fresh flat-leaf parsley

Salt, black pepper, and cayenne to taste

Clean the crabmeat of shells.

In a medium bowl, whip the egg lightly, then add the crab, Dijon, Worcestershire, aïoli, and crushed crackers. Season with Tabasco, lemon juice, and salt and pepper to taste.

Form 4-ounce crab cakes and pan-fry in oil over medium-high heat about 3½ minutes per side, until golden brown.

Serve with aïoli.

robert luna

Growing up in the Boyle Heights section of Los Angeles, Chef Robert Luna developed a culinary appreciation at an early age, as his mother invented a new dish each evening for dinner for the family to taste. It was these dishes that eventually had a hand in inspiring Chef Luna to develop some of Malo and Mas Malo's most popular menu items. One of those early favorite family inventions was his mother's ground beef tacos, which is currently the best-selling item on the menu at both locations. Luna's mother inspired him to create his own take on home-style Mexican cooking, and after high school, Luna attended Tri-Tech Culinary School and began his culinary career.

Luna was former executive chef at Cobras y Matadors in Los Angeles. His work there garnered him much acclaim.

Today, Chef Luna heads up Malo Cantina Suavacita in Los Angeles' Silver Lake neighborhood, as well as Mas Malo downtown. Focused on sourcing the best local and organic proteins, dairy, and produce, Luna is bringing a sustainable approach to creative Mexican cooking.

ground beef
and pickle taco

1 pound ground beef
¼ cup olive oil
1 teaspoon garlic powder
1 teaspoon ground cumin
1 teaspoon dried oregano
2 tablespoons paprika
Salt and pepper to taste
2 russet potatoes, boiled and cut into small dice
Soft corn tortillas
1 cup canola oil, for frying
8 ounces cheddar cheese, grated
Pickle chips

Sauté the beef in the oil over medium heat for about 3 minutes. The meat should still be a little pink at this point—not fully cooked.

Add all the dry spices and cook 5 minutes. Add the potatoes. Continue to cook another 8 to 10 minutes. Remove from heat and let cool on the counter for 30 minutes.

Heat the corn tortillas and fill them with the beef and potato mixture. Close both ends with a toothpick.

Heat the canola oil, then fry the tortillas in the oil about 2 minutes on each side. When done, place on paper towels, remove the toothpicks, open each tortilla, and add cheddar cheese and pickle chips.

salvatore marino

A second-generation restaurateur, Sal Marino is chef and owner of Il Grano in West L.A., where he brings a lifelong passion and craftsmanship of the cuisine to the kitchen. He gained experience cooking alongside his father, Ciro Marino, and then working throughout the Italian peninsula in all manner of local eateries, including Gualtiero Marchesi and Tomavento.

Inspired by the food of southern Italy where he grew up, Marino is best known for his high-quality seafood and seasonal menus. His motto might be stated as "Sharing the love of food with staff and customers, committed to deliver enjoyment with food prepared with passion."

Marino is part of the family-owned Marino Ristorante in Hollywood and co-owner of La Bottega Marino in Larchmont Village and Beverly Hills.

caramelle di burrata e pomodorini

MAKES 4 SERVINGS

Pasta

8 ounces semolina

7 eggs

¼ cup water

Pinch of salt

4 ounces all-purpose flour, for dusting

or

Fresh pasta sheets purchased at a pasta store
   (enough for 18 4 × 5-inch rectangles)

Filling

1 pound burrata cheese

1 tablespoon chopped fresh flat-leaf Italian parsley

1 teaspoon extra-virgin olive oil

Salt and pepper

Sauce

4 garlic cloves

¼ cup extra-virgin olive oil

1 pound ripe cherry, pear, or Sweet 100 tomatoes
   or 28 ounces canned cherry tomatoes
   ("Pomodorini del Vesuvio")

1 stalk fresh basil plus torn basil leaves for garnish

Sea salt and freshly ground black pepper to taste

Some notes before you begin:

> If you're making this recipe during the summer months, use the ripe, sweet cherry tomatoes, not the firm ones used in salad. They don't make good sauce as they don't have enough liquid. (If good tomatoes are not in season, the canned tomatoes are preferable.)

> Use the best extra-virgin olive oil. This dish is simple; don't use a cooking olive oil.

> If you can't get sea salt or fleur de sel, use coarse kosher salt.

> Grind the pepper in a pepper mill; do not use the preground kind. You lose aroma and intensity.

> Keep the burrata refrigerated.

Make the Pasta: Place the semolina flour and 6 egg yolks in a stand mixer and start mixing on slow speed. (Save the whites for another purpose.) Slowly add the water as the dough becomes more solid and comes together as one piece. Add a pinch of salt. When done, cover with a cloth and allow to rest for 10 to 20 minutes.

While the dough is resting, start the filling and prepare the sauce; then come back to make the caramelle. You'll have everything ready in less than an hour.

Sprinkle the all-purpose flour over your work surface and rolling pin so the dough won't stick. With the rolling pin, stretch out your pasta dough to a thin layer—it should be a bit thinner than a commercially purchased lasagna noodle. Cut the pasta sheets into eighteen 4x5-inch rectangles. (You should have 2 extra.)

Make the Filling: Cut the burrata into large cubes. Using a slotted spoon, mix the cheese and parsley in a bowl, pressing down to form a compact mixture. Add the olive oil and salt and pepper to taste.

Make the Sauce: Peel and gently crack the garlic cloves, but keep in one piece. Heat the oil in a large saucepan and sauté the garlic in the oil until golden brown. Pour the tomatoes (if using canned tomatoes, include the juice) into the pan, and start breaking them up with a spoon. Toss in the stalk of basil. Lower the heat to low and cook for 10 minutes. Add salt and pepper to taste and cook until sauce has reduced to the desired consistency.

Assemble the Caramelle: Divide the filling into 18 balls and place a spoonful on each rectangle on the 5-inch side. Beat the remaining egg and brush the four corners of the pasta. Roll the pasta into a cylinder, keeping the stuffing in the middle. Close the two ends shut, pressing hard against the table, and gently seal the length of the caramelle by brushing with more egg wash and applying some pressure along the seal and a little pinch. Now squeeze both ends of the pasta separately, twisting slightly to give the impression of a wrapped candy. Your caramelle are done. Place in a dish lined with parchment paper or enough semolina flour so that the pasta doesn't stick.

Bring a large pot of salted water to a boil. Place the caramelle in the water one by one, being careful that they don't break. Boil for 4 to 5 minutes, until the middle of the caramelle begins to soften; it will no longer hold a stiff cylindrical shape.

Using a slotted spoon, transfer the caramelle one by one to the pan with the tomato sauce and cook together for a couple of minutes. Don't stir too much or the filling will break. Sprinkle with fresh basil.

Pour some sauce on the bottom of the plate, carefully set the caramelle over the sauce, and serve.

Buon appetito!

michael mccarty

Blurring the lines between inventor, art collector, entrepreneur, vintner, and chef, Michael McCarty has left an unmistakable impression on the food world with his legendary Michael's restaurants in New York and Santa Monica, California. Often known as the father of California cuisine, Michael McCarty remains a driving force and inspiration in featuring local and seasonal produce, meats, and fish in his ever-flavorful cuisine today.

Michael's studies at home and abroad led him to develop and hone a cuisine that became his own. Michael McCarty opened Michael's in Santa Monica in 1979 at the age of twenty-five. An instant success, it remains one of the most acclaimed and popular restaurants in the United States. A decade after the Santa Monica debut, Michael's New York opened in Midtown Manhattan.

duck confit salad

courtesy of executive chef mikey stern

MAKES 2 SERVINGS

Pickled Onions

1 red onion, thinly sliced

½ cup red wine vinegar

1 tablespoon grapeseed oil

Sugar and salt to taste

Salad

2 legs/thighs prepared duck confit (available at specialty food markets; see Note)

2 tablespoons grapeseed oil

3 bunches frisée, coarsely chopped

1 bunch arugula, stems removed

¼ cup pickled onion (see recipe below)

8 ounces blue cheese, crumbled

Salt and pepper to taste

1 tablespoon olive oil

Saba to taste (see Note)

Make the Pickled Onions: Combine all the ingredients and mix well.

Make the Duck: Debone the duck and shred the meat. Heat a medium-sized sauté pan over medium heat. Pour in the grapeseed oil. Add the duck to the hot pan and sauté until crispy. Set aside.

Meanwhile, toss together the greens, onions, blue cheese, and salt and pepper. Drizzle with olive oil and saba to taste. Top with the warm duck and serve immediately.

Note: Saba can be purchased at European markets. Chinese roast duck can be substituted for the duck confit.

joe miller

After graduating from the Culinary Institute of America in Hyde Park, New York, Joe Miller headed to Los Angeles. He then worked in several restaurants, including La Toque, Patina, and L'Orangerie, but he received his first recognition as a chef at Café Katsu in Los Angeles. In keeping with Café Katsu's intimate, casual style, he next opted to open a neighborhood restaurant serving French–California cuisine at affordable prices. Miller, along with members of his original staff at Café Katsu, worked diligently, and within only a month of renovating the space on Abbot Kinney Boulevard in Venice, California, opened the doors to Joe's Restaurant in September 2001. Consistently rated by the Zagat Survey as one of the top ten restaurants in Los Angeles, Joe's Restaurant has earned numerous positive reviews by major publications in Los Angeles and throughout the United States.

Chef Miller, a visionary in the kitchen, says the secret of Joe's cuisine is the result of mixing formal French techniques with Asian and California-influenced esthetics and by using only the best ingredients. In addition to frequenting local farmer's markets, Miller searches out regional items from around the country and even around the world. He is constantly looking for new trends and influences in cuisine that he can recreate in his kitchen.

Miller says that his philosophy has remained the same since he opened his doors—to create innovative, yet reasonably priced dishes in a warm, elegant atmosphere. Miller believes that dining at Joe's is an experience where all the elements, from the food and wine to impeccable service, are key to the entire experience.

tuna tartar

Preserved Lemon

4 medium lemons, cut into wedges

⅔ cup kosher salt

1 cup lemon juice

1 cup extra-virgin olive oil

Tuna

1 pound Ahi tuna (sushi grade #2)

1 teaspoon mayonnaise

1½ teaspoons green peppercorns in brine, drained

2 preserved lemons (make these in advance)

1 tablespoon finely diced yellow onion, plus 2 tablespoons for serving

2 tablespoons drained capers

2 tablespoons finely chopped fresh chives

1 tablespoon finely diced shallot

2 tablespoons finely chopped fresh parsley

1 teaspoon extra-virgin olive oil

Lemon juice to taste

Salt and pepper to taste

2 ounces smoked salmon, sliced

1 hothouse cucumber, finely sliced

2 Roma tomatoes, diced

Make the Preserved Lemon: Place all ingredients in a jar with a tight lid and let sit at room temperature for 7 days. Shake well every day.

Prepare the Tuna: Clean the tuna and cut into small dice. Mix the mayonnaise and green peppercorns. Cut the preserved lemons into small wedges.

In a bowl, mix the tuna, onion, capers, chives, shallots, and parsley. Add the olive oil and mayonnaise. Mix lightly to blend. Season with lemon juice, salt, and pepper.

In the center of a plate, place a layer of smoked salmon. Place a ball of tuna tartar on top. Add a preserved lemon wedge and some cucumber, then sprinkle tomatoes and extra diced onion around the plate.

david myers

David Myers is a renowned Los Angeles–based chef who captivated the attention of the culinary world in 2002 with his Michelin-starred Sona, followed by one of Los Angeles' first modern French brasseries, Comme Ça, and an Italian neighborhood-inspired Pizzeria Ortica in Orange County. Myers founded David Myers Group, which owns and operates the restaurants in addition to two concepts that debuted in fall 2010 in the Ginza district of Tokyo: a high-end patisserie called SOLA, which has since added an additional SOLA location in Isetan Shinjuku, and David Myers Café, showcasing California-inspired cuisine with Japanese ingredients. Myers made his first foray into Las Vegas in late 2010 with Comme Ça at The Cosmopolitan of Las Vegas, and his culinary capabilities have been widely recognized, culminating in notable accolades such as Food & Wine's "Best New Chefs" and Angelino's "Man of Style."

vanilla hazelnut pancakes with toasted pistachios, fresh berries, and whipped cream

MAKES 20 SERVINGS

Pancakes

3¼ cups all-purpose flour
2 cups hazelnut flour
1½ tablespoons baking powder
1½ cups vanilla sugar
1 tablespoon kosher salt
10 eggs
2 tablespoons canola oil

Whipped Cream

2¼ cups heavy whipping cream
1 cup confectioners' sugar
¼ cup orange zest

1 cup toasted finely chopped pistachios
1½ cups fresh berries of your choosing

Whip the Cream: Pour the heavy whipping cream into a chilled mixing bowl and whip to soft peaks. Add the sugar and zest and continue whipping to stiff peaks. Put into a piping bag.

Make the Pancakes: Combine the dry ingredients in a mixing bowl, add all the wet ingredients, and whip until fully incorporated.

Heat a griddle until hot. For each pancake, pour ¼ cup of batter onto the griddle. When bubbles appear on the surface, flip the pancake and continue cooking until golden brown. Serve immediately with the toppings.

To Serve: Place one pancake per plate, top with a quenelle of whipped cream, and garnish with a generous tablespoon of fresh berries and a sprinkle of the pistachios.

larry nicola

Larry Nicola's love affair with food began when he was a young child at his family's Nicola Twins Market in Silver Lake, where he grew up. In July 1980, Nicola opened his first restaurant, L.A. Nicola, across the street from his family's market, defining L.A. Nicola as one of Silver Lake's first serious dining establishments. A few years later, Nicola, both chef and owner, expanded L.A. Nicola to include the first martini lounge in this area of Los Angeles, and it was the mix of bar, lounge, restaurant, music, and atmosphere created by Nicola that made L.A. Nicola one of L.A.'s best restaurants.

In 1993, Nicola ventured downtown with a new restaurant, aptly titled Nicola, and in 1997 he decided to move his restaurant "halfway between Silver Lake and Venice" to Beverly Hills, where he opened Nic's Beverly Hills.

In 2006 Larry Nicola created Vodbox, which is the ultimate "walk-in, drink-in" 28-degree, exhibition vodka-tasting freezer designed for tasting flights of vodkas in their purest form. The Vodbox became an instant hit and one of L.A.'s most unique bar experiences, offering visitors—who don faux fur coats while sipping pure vodka—flights of rare, premium, and luxury vodkas from all over the world.

morita-crusted ahi tartare butter lettuce cups with habanero nasturtium drizzle

MAKES 4 SERVINGS (2 PIECES EACH)

Prepare the Chile Mix: Preheat the oven to 350°F. Crack open the morita chiles and remove the seeds. Place in a pan and roast until charred and crisp, approximately 30 minutes. Let cool, then crush into flakes and blend with the Shichimi Togarashi Mix. Set aside.

Make the Habanero Oil: Meanwhile, put the habanero chiles, tomato, and garlic in another baking pan, drizzle with the tablespoon of olive oil, and season with salt and pepper.

Cook in a 350°F oven for about 45 minutes, or until the habaneros and tomato are fully browned and roasted. (This can be done at the same time as the morita chiles, but not in the same pan.)

Place the habanero mix in a blender and add the extra-virgin olive oil, green onions, cilantro, and nasturtium and blend until smooth. Add salt and pepper to taste.

Make the Tuna Dressing: Mix together the dressing ingredients and set aside.

Prepare the Tuna: Heat the olive oil in a skillet. Dredge the tuna in the morita chile flakes on 2 sides and sear lightly until slightly crisp and browned. Let cool, chop roughly, and toss with the dressing.

Place the butter lettuce leaves on a plate. Divide the tuna between the lettuce cups. Top with sliced avocado and pickled ginger and drizzle with habanero oil. Salt and pepper to taste.

Chile Mix

2 dried morita chiles
1 tablespoon Japanese Shichimi Togarashi Mix (can be purchased at any Japanese grocery store)

Habanero Oil

2 habanero chiles, stems and seeds removed (wear gloves!)
1 medium heirloom tomato, sliced in half
1 garlic clove, chopped
1 tablespoon olive oil
Salt and pepper to taste
¼ cup extra-virgin olive oil
2 green onions, roughly chopped
¼ bunch cilantro (use stems and leaves)
8 nasturtium leaves

Tuna Dressing

2 tablespoons sesame oil
1 tablespoon soy sauce
1 tablespoon grated fresh ginger
¼ cup extra-virgin olive oil
Salt and pepper to taste

Tuna

2 tablespoons olive oil, for searing
1½ pounds Ahi tuna steak (approximately 1½ inches thick)
8 butter lettuce leaves

Garnish

1 avocado, sliced
½ cup pickled ginger

mirko paderno

Growing up in Milan, Oliverio executive chef Mirko Paderno began his journey at the Cesare Ritz School in Merano, where his interest in Italian cuisine flourished.

At the Four Seasons Hotel in Milan, Paderno developed a style that focused on the flavor of the food above all else, and in 1999, he took that style to Los Angeles, where he assumed the role of executive chef at Piero Selvaggio's restaurant, Primi.

In the decade since, Paderno has lent his skills to some of the city's most famed Italian kitchens, including Valentino, Celestino Drago, All'Angelo (which was named one of the city's best new restaurants by Esquire *magazine during his tenure), and Cecconi's, before settling at Oliverio in fall 2009.*

Dough

½ ounce fresh yeast
2½ tablespoons lukewarm water
1¾ ounces cooked potatoes, riced
4 ounces Barilla 00 flour
Pinch of salt
2 cups olive oil, for frying

Topping

2 tablespoons tomato sauce
1 ounce grated Parmigiano-Reggiano
2 ounces burrata cheese
2 basil leaves

pizzetta fritta napoletana

MAKES 1 SERVING

Dissolve the yeast in the lukewarm water. Add the riced potato, flour, and salt to form a dough. Work the dough on a floured counter to get an elastic dough. Place in a bowl, cover with plastic wrap, and let rest for a couple hours, until doubled in size.

Preheat the oven to 450°F.

Roll the dough to an 8-inch diameter. Fry in olive oil over high heat until golden brown on both sides. Transfer to a baking sheet.

Spread the tomato sauce over the pizza dough and cover with Parmigiano. Bake for 5 minutes, until the dough is crispy. Cut the burrata into pieces and place on the pizza, followed by torn basil. Cut the pizza into slices and serve.

t. nicolas peter

For over fifteen years, Chef T. Nicolas Peter has presented simple and elegant French Mediterranean fare at The Little Door and Little Next Door, creating menus that showcase his natural talent for creating harmonious dishes that balance the ingredients' flavor, texture, color, and consistency. Captured by the aromas of fresh produce, herbs, and spices, Chef Peter carefully considers the flavor of each ingredient when developing a new dish, and is always refining familiar entrées to keep surprising and pleasing palates.

tzatziki sauce

Peel, seed, and shred the cucumbers, then add the salt. Set aside in a colander for about 20 minutes.

In a large bowl, mix all the other ingredients until smooth.

Wrap the shredded cucumber in cheesecloth and squeeze out as much excess liquid as possible.

Add the cucumber to the other ingredients and mix thoroughly. Check for salt, cayenne, and lemon juice and adjust the seasoning as needed.

4 large cucumbers
1 tablespoon sea salt
1½ cups Greek yogurt
2 teaspoons chopped garlic
Juice from 1½ lemons
1½ tablespoons chopped fresh dill
1½ tablespoons chopped fresh mint
¼ cup extra-virgin olive oil
Pinch of cayenne pepper

akasha richmond

Akasha Richmond is a self-trained chef and artisan-style baker who has been catering events in Los Angeles and other parts of the country for over twenty years. She began her professional career at the Golden Temple, a now defunct but once popular vegetarian restaurant in Los Angeles. It was in this kitchen that Akasha discovered her passion for making delicious dishes with good-for-you ingredients. Akasha is her first restaurant venture, the result of a vision she has had for many years.

Her cookbook Hollywood Dish *includes tales of Hollywood's hundred-year passion for organic foods and healthy lifestyles and stories of her favorite cooking experiences: making holiday dinners for Billy Bob Thornton, catering parties for Pierce Brosnan, producing events at the Sundance Film Festival, and working as a private chef for Barbra Streisand.*

cinnamon french toast with POM apple compote

MAKES 4 SERVINGS

POM Apple Compote

Juice from 2 to 3 large POM Wonderful
   pomegranates (see Note) or 1 cup POM
   Wonderful 100% pomegranate juice
1 vanilla bean, cut lengthwise
½ cup dried, pitted cherries
1 tablespoon unsalted butter
2 pounds Gala apples, peeled and sliced
   ½ inch thick
½ cup pure maple syrup

Cinnamon French Toast

4 large eggs
1¼ cups low-fat milk or plain soy milk
1 tablespoon vanilla extract
½ teaspoon ground cinnamon
¼ teaspoon grated fresh nutmeg
8 slices cinnamon swirl or challah bread, sliced
   1½ inches thick
2 tablespoons unsalted butter

Garnish

1 cup arils from 1 or 2 large POM Wonderful
   pomegranates
Confectioners' sugar as needed

Make the POM Apple Compote: Prepare the fresh pomegranate juice (see Note). Heat the pomegranate juice in a small saucepan over medium heat until it simmers.

Turn off the heat; add the vanilla bean and dried cherries. Let rest for 15 minutes, until cherries are plump. Scrape the vanilla beans out of the pod and add them back into the compote; discard the remaining pod.

Heat a 12-inch skillet over medium-high heat. Melt the butter in the pan and add the sliced apples. Cook the apples until they begin to soften but still hold their shape, 5 to 6 minutes.

Add the maple syrup to the apples along with the pomegranate juice and cherries. Simmer until the juice reduces to syrup, 5 to 8 minutes. Keep warm.

Make the Cinnamon French Toast: Score 1 or 2 fresh pomegranates and place in a bowl of water. Break open the pomegranates under water to free the arils (seed sacs). The arils will sink to the bottom of the bowl and the membrane will float to the top. Sieve and put the arils in a separate bowl. Reserve 1 cup of the arils and set aside. (Refrigerate or freeze remaining arils for another use.)

In a large bowl, whisk together the eggs, milk (or soy milk), vanilla extract, cinnamon, and nutmeg.

Place the bread slices in a single layer in a casserole dish and cover with the egg mixture. Let soak for 5 to 10 minutes.

Melt 2 tablespoons of butter in a 12-inch nonstick skillet over medium-high heat. Add the slices of soaked bread to the pan and cook until golden brown, about 4 minutes per side.

Top the French toast with the warm compote. Sprinkle with confectioners' sugar and garnish with the fresh pomegranate arils.

Note: For 1 cup of juice, cut 2 or 3 large POM Wonderful pomegranates in half and juice them with a citrus reamer or juicer. Pour the mixture through a cheesecloth-lined strainer or sieve. Set the juice aside.

robert sarstedt

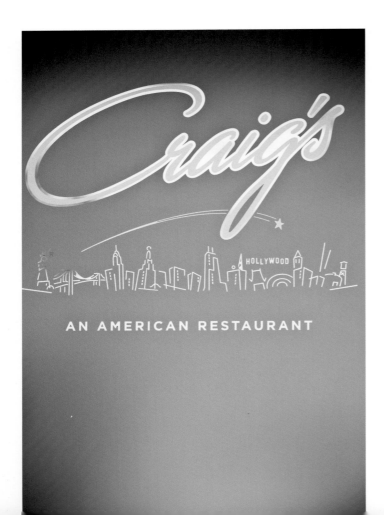

AN AMERICAN RESTAURANT

Robert Sarstedt grew up in Los Angeles but has also lived and studied in San Francisco, Las Vegas, and Phoenix. While working in post production, he developed a passion for cooking and attended Le Cordon Bleu in San Francisco and Las Vegas. After graduating, he spent time at Daniel Boulud Brasserie in Las Vegas but eventually ended up back in Los Angeles.

On returning home, Robert worked at BOA Steakhouse, Spago, and Il Sole; he was formerly the head chef of Taste on Melrose in West Hollywood. Robert is now the executive chef at Craig's in West Hollywood. He possesses a remarkable ability to create and retain the individual character of each of his endeavors, insisting on uniqueness and integrity.

bbq ribs

10 quarts water
½ cup liquid smoke
5 tablespoons garlic powder
5 tablespoons onion powder
5 tablespoons Cajun seasoning
5 racks baby back pork ribs

Pour the water and liquid smoke into a large roasting pan set across two burners. Combine the spices in a mixing bowl. Add half the spice mixture to the water. Place the ribs in the water and cover. Bring the water to a boil, then simmer for 1½ hours or until tender.

When the ribs are tender, drain them and let cool. Preheat the oven to 350°F. When the ribs are cool enough to touch, rub them with the remaining spice mixture.

Return the ribs to the roasting pan and place in the oven for 20 minutes to let the rub penetrate the meat.

deborah schneider

Deborah Schneider left a cushy magazine editing job to cook on yachts in the Mediterranean and Florida before moving to San Diego, where she has run some of the city's best (and biggest) kitchens. Deborah is currently is executive chef/partner of SOL Cocina in Newport Beach. She is the author of four cookbooks, including Amor y Tacos, ¡Baja! Cooking on the Edge, *and the James Beard–nominated* Cooking with the Seasons at Rancho La Puerta.

carnitas SOL (shredded pork with tomatillo salsa and crunchy pork skin on a tortilla)

MAKES 6–8 SERVINGS (24 STREET-SIZE TACOS)

Cook the Pork: Preheat the oven to 325°F. Cut the pork into 3-inch chunks and place in a baking dish just large enough to hold the meat in one layer. Toss the meat with salt and add 1 inch of water. Wrap the dish with foil and cook for 2½ hours, or until the meat is very tender when poked with a sharp knife.

Poke a hole in the foil and cool the meat in the stock for 30 minutes. Remove large pieces of fat and break up the meat with 2 forks, not too small. The carnitas may be eaten immediately or chilled and reheated.

Make the Tomatillo Salsa: In a food processor, pulse the tomatillos until they form a chunky puree. Add the onion, serrano chile, cilantro, and salt, and pulse to make a chunky, thick puree.

Taste for salt and add more as needed. Use immediately. If the tomatillos are very juicy, drain off some of the liquid that forms in the salsa.

To Serve: Pile the meat into warm corn tortillas. Top with tomatillo salsa, avocado, a couple of small pieces of chicharrón, and some white onion and cilantro. The best!

Pork

3 pounds boneless pork shoulder or country-style pork ribs, with fat left on
1 teaspoon kosher salt
Warm corn tortillas
Tomatillo Salsa
Diced avocado

Tomatillo Salsa

6 medium tomatillos, husked and washed
½ cup diced white onion (about half a small onion)
1 large serrano chile, stemmed
12 sprigs cilantro, stemmed (¼ cup packed leaves)
½ teaspoon kosher salt, or more to taste

Chicharrón (fried pork skin), broken up
Diced white onion
Chopped cilantro

rainer schwarz

Rainer Schwarz brings his own rich cultural past and diverse culinary training to Public Kitchen & Bar, Hollywood Roosevelt Hotel, as executive chef. With past experience in operations, systems, training, and management, and a mastery of culinary skills accrued over almost three decades of worldwide practice, Schwarz has an eclectic background that has led him to believe that less is more—boasting a deceptively simple and eclectic American menu.

Pesto

2 cups cubed country bread

½ cup water

2 cups fresh flat-leaf parsley leaves

1 cup olive oil

1 teaspoon capers

4 anchovy fillets

½ teaspoon salt

1½ pounds burrata cheese, cut into small pieces
   (you should have about 3⅓ cups)

1 cluster cherry tomatoes on the vine or 1 pint

Sea salt to taste

Lemon oil to taste

burrata cheese in a glass

MAKES 10 SERVINGS

Combine all the pesto ingredients in a food
processor and blend until semi-smooth.

To assemble, place ¼ cup of pesto in a clear
glass, add ⅓ cup of burrata, and top with
2 or 3 cherry tomatoes. Sprinkle with salt and
drizzle with a few drops of lemon oil.

jon shook and vinny dotolo

Jon Shook and Vinny Dotolo opened
Animal restaurant in June 2008 to
widespread acclaim. In the almost
two years since opening its doors, the
duo has been awarded Food & Wine
magazine's Best New Chefs of 2009,
received a James Beard nomination
for Best New Restaurant, and most
recently been named Rising Star Chefs
by Starchefs.com. Jon and Vinny met
while attending culinary school at
the Art Institute of Fort Lauderdale
in Florida and from there, their first
job together was in the kitchen of
famed chef Michelle Bernstein at The
Strand restaurant in South Beach.
In the years since, they have worked
in many renowned restaurants
and launched a successful catering
endeavor that ultimately led them to
opening their first restaurant, Animal.

chorizo

10 pounds pork shoulder, diced
¼ cup chopped garlic
2 tablespoons sweet paprika
2 tablespoons onion powder
1 tablespoon garlic salt
¼ cup garlic powder
1 tablespoon cayenne pepper
1 tablespoon ground ginger
1½ cups golden raisins
1 cup toasted almonds
2 tablespoons ground cumin
2 tablespoons ground coriander
2 tablespoons chili powder
2 tablespoons ancho chile powder
2 tablespoons chipotle chile powder
1 tablespoon black pepper
¼ cup salt

Season the meat with all the ingredients. Put through the grinder twice.

Shape the chorizo into patties and grill or sear. You can also break up the chorizo and mix it in hash or tacos.

Sherry Yard's passion for baking was born in her grandmother's Brooklyn kitchen, where she remembers having suppers of spaghetti and ice cream floats. Her education at New York City Technical College and the Culinary Institute of America led her to New York City's top restaurants, including the Rainbow Room, Montrachet, and the Tribeca Grill. She moved west to command the pastry kitchen at San Francisco's Campton Place Restaurant and then to Napa Valley to Jan Birnbaum's Catahoula as pastry chef. Sherry joined Spago Hollywood as pastry chef in 1994.

Sherry was named Pastry Chef of the Year for 1998–1999 by the Southern California Restaurants Writers' Association, Bon Appétit's Pastry Chef of the Year for 2000, and after four previous nominations, claimed the James Beard Foundation's Outstanding Pastry Chef of the Year for 2002. She has created show-stopping desserts for the Grammy Awards, the Emmy Awards, and for the last eight Governors' Ball dinners following the Academy Awards broadcast.

Sherry is on the board of directors of the Women Chefs & Restaurateurs organization and is active in the Careers Through Culinary Arts Program, which educates inner-city children and gives scholarships to culinary schools. She is also personally involved in the Meals on Wheels program in Los Angeles.

sherry yard

In a large stainless steel mixing bowl set over a hot water bath, whisk the raspberry marmalade smooth to 60°F. Add the lemon juice. Reserve.

Preheat the oven to 375°F.

Create an Italian meringue: In the bowl of a standing electric mixer fitted with a whip attachment, begin to whip all the egg whites on low speed.

Meanwhile, in a heavy metal saucepan, stir together the 4¼ ounces sugar and the water. Set over high heat and cook to 235°F—NO HIGHER! This will take 5 minutes.

When the sugar comes to a boil, turn the mixer to medium speed, whipping the egg whites to a foam. Add the cream of tartar and 1 tablespoon sugar.

When the sugar reaches 235°F, remove from heat, allowing the bubbles to disperse.

With the mixer still on medium speed, carefully stream the hot sugar into the soft whipped meringue. Continue whipping for 1 minute, until the meringue has cooled slightly and tripled in size.

With a balloon whip, fold half of the whipped whites into the soufflé base. With a rubber spatula, fold in the balance of egg whites and the raspberries or chocolate.

Fill a disposable piping bag with the soufflé batter and cut a tip 1 inch wide. Starting from the bottom of each ramekin, pipe to the top. With a palette knife or offset spatula, smooth the top. Bake for 15 minutes.

Garnish with the reserved marmalade and serve.

raspberry chocolate chip soufflé

MAKES EIGHT 6-OUNCE RAMEKINS

6 ounces raspberry marmalade

1 tablespoon lemon juice

4¼ ounces (heaping ½ cup) sugar, plus 1 tablespoon

1 tablespoon water

6 egg whites

¼ teaspoon cream of tartar

6 ounces fresh raspberries or 8 ounces bittersweet chocolate, cut into ½-inch pieces

index of recipes